Dissecting the Angel

DISSECTING

THE

ANGEL

and other poems

MICHELLE CASTLEBERRY

MIGLIOR PRESS

ATHENS, GEORGIA

Published by Miglior Press
P. O. Box 7487
Athens, Georgia 30604

www.migliorpress.com

Several of these poems have previously appeared in *Umbrella, Bellemeade Books, The Dead Mule School of Southern Literature, Poemeleon, The Southern Poetry Anthology, Volume V: Georgia,* and *The Chattahoochee Review.*

ISBN 978-0-9836484-4-4

Printed in the United States of America

First edition

With gratitude to Aralee Strange
and the Word of Mouth community,
where I found my heart and my home.

Contents

About the Author

Acknowledgements

Preface

The Poem I Want to Write

Every year the poem I most want to write . . . changes shapes,
changes directions . . . my splendid catch.

—C. D. Wright

The poem I want to write
is one you want to follow
if only at first for the odd music it makes,
like a fiddle-tune caught in the treetops.
Even when it leads you into a dark wooded hollow,
and night has come, and you have on Sunday shoes.

The poem tells your worst, most secret, wish.
It is written in pokeberry juice,
in the invisible ink of spit on a lover's thigh,
written in blood and keloid. It is the rusted lockbox
and also the glinting, silver key.

The poem I want to write is a poltergeist.
I have heard it breaking windows and furniture,
heard it making howls just beyond the door.
I sit with a tape recorder, pen, and notebook for science.
I keep holy water and a crucifix nearby for safety.

After a thirteen-hour road trip,
standing in the kitchen feeling like you left yourself
at some gas station bathroom on I-20,
the poem is the drink of water
that sinks you back into yourself, and thusly, the world.

The poem I most want to write is like this:
One night when I was seventeen, my brother and father
woke me after a late trap run.

The cold was damp and shard-y in my lungs
as I walked toward the halogen lights in the yard.
Across the ATV, draped in its own fading warmth,
was a dead bobcat. I touched the black tufted ears,
spread the pads of his enormous paws.
He had a knot on one leg from a healed fracture
and faded scars on his face.
We could have been the same age.
I left the men, incandescent in their pride,
to go cry in the starred dark behind the house.

If I ever meet the poem I want to write,
I am uncertain if I will take it down
or kneel at its blessing and watch it pass.

Dissecting the Angel
and Other Poems

Dissecting the Angel

To solve the problem of how to make the subject lie flat
the wings were cut off, now an angled pile in the corner.
Not white, but the same dun color as the wrens
whose nest the coroner knocked from the eaves that morning.
The torso made a curved bridge over a back of knotted muscles
like crepe myrtle limbs.
Arms and legs surprisingly thin.
He cracked the ribcage like a shell
and stumbled back from the smell of incense.

Thirty-four years of experience and a Quaker upbringing
pulled him up from the floor. "Hands to work."
He started with the known and familiar,
the body a child's counting game:
Here ten fingers and toes, there four limbs,
the spongy twin bellows of lungs,
the single muscled ball of heart, enlarged.
Then he was lost.

Below the waist a juncture
that bore both bud and seam,
either too pronounced or too subtle to signify.
His pen hovered over the boxes—*M, F.*
He peered into the face for clues.
Nothing came but a song, forgotten since '65,
a girl named Eileen, her sugar-sweet perfume,
and a very specific tension in his own torso.
He cleared his throat, chalked it up to proof
of nothing more than the ability to see beauty.

He washed his instruments of the blood
so like dandelion juice, glanced at the brain

shivering and translucent in the silver tray,
fought the urge to taste it.
He tried again to complete his form:

Subject name: Unknown.
Date of Birth: Before
Race: Translucent
Sex: Inward and outward, only and every
Date of Death: Last night when the lights blinked
and a streak of light smeared the sky
Cause of Death:

Here, the coroner stopped writing
and opened the angel's mouth,
kept it propped with the tanned cartilage
of his own right ear.

The daughter found him like this, whispering,
"Tell me, Messenger, tell me."

Woman on Fire

in memory of Lisa Davenport

I.

The burn unit in Herat, Afghanistan
fills with women, at times ten deep.
The air vibrates with cries, is thick and singed.
Girls wrapped in bandages of bridal white
tremble with arms charred at right angles,
lifted to hold, lifted to praise nothing.
Most of them set themselves alight.

What makes a woman combustible?
What makes her soak her dress in kerosene
and drop a match at her feet?

Where there is no tenderness or hope,
where there is no warmth or light,
Even the poorest homes
have matches and cooking oil.

What makes a woman catch fire?
Where there is no tenderness or hope,
where there is no warmth . . .

Have a girl-child, beat a cadence
into her skin and sing a chorus
of negations over the drum of her body.
When she turns twelve,
marry her off to settle a debt
to a man of fifty who takes up the dark song.
Fill her with children,

fill her with words like guttering embers.
Pack them in every day until you smell her.
If you watch, you can see her flare.
Then ignite.

Where there is no tenderness or hope . . .
Even the poorest homes
have matches and cooking oil.
Where there is no warmth or light,
women burst into flame.

In a portrait of a survivor,
the flame is there still,
in whorls of flesh resembling abalone,
in a scrim of scar tissue like wax.
Her eyes burn out at you
with something like pride, saying
"This body is beautiful
because it is mine."

II.

A woman is a landscape.
Her body is a map.
A man can be cartographer,
explorer, realtor, or lover of the land.

A woman is a landscape.
Her body is a map.
Some men see a mountain
and fall to their knees
happy, humbled by its beauty.

Others see a mountain
and want to take the top off
to get at the vein of coal inside.

Some see a woman
(A woman is a landscape
Her body . . .)
and talk of acreage, of property lines.
When they learn they cannot own her,
they salt the earth, burn the map,
set fire to a wooded lot
and cross the street to watch it burn.

Here the comparison breaks down.
If you destroy a woman to mine her heart,
she will escape with it every time,
even into death.

A woman is a landscape.
Her body is a map.

What are you?

III.

Take them back.
The words "woman on fire."
Take them back
. . . make them metaphor again.

Where there is tenderness
let a woman warm herself

in the shell-light of an embrace,
in the dawn-light of a child's face.

She is a landscape named home.
Her body is a map
of heaven pulled down
for those brave enough to see.
Where there is hope
let a woman kindle visions,
fan a spark of resistance
to lead a people.
There is warmth in a woman
loved well from birth, cast out in rays
as palpable as breath.

If a woman is on fire (say it)
let her burn with a poem or song
that troubles her sleep until
it scorches the page and air.
If a woman is ablaze
let her burn from the furnace of her desire
stoked under the gaze of her lover.
Let both of them find her beautiful.

Where there is tenderness,
and warmth, and hope and light
for every girl-child,
where there is tenderness,
and warmth, and hope and light—
every woman can burn
and none will perish.

Joan of Arc

Prayer is not posing,
not meant to be seen.
Not the way I do it,
eyes rolled up, chin pulled down,
wracked, rictus.

Hear me.

I offer ugliness as my sacrifice,
myself made odd and misshapen,
sore from locked muscles,
neck spit-slick.

Oh, hear me.

No, I do not look like the pictures
or sculptures, so pretty,
a girl in soldier-boy drag,
caught listening.
If you saw me pray,
if you saw me fight,
you would understand.

Lead me.

When the jailers took my shell
and split it where it seamed,
I laughed down on them
from the corner of the ceiling.
They thought they were punishing me
for trying to be a man.

Why would I bother?
Sex is too little for what I am.

From above them, from within her,
I pray for what they cannot do.

God me.

Possum Prayer

Let my pelt stay cheap
at one dollar a hide.
Bless the grin, greed-wide.
Though dim-sighted
and stuff-eared, let my pink
skin shine from snout
and nailbed. Let them see
the part that looks like them.
Hiss-cursing them
that curse the tail
from the rat of their nightmares.
Dear god of rank forest bottom,
bring us the reek of plenty.

The Shape of an Animal

for C.

Beautiful books, the width of a fist
strapped open in a glass case,
each vellum page formerly a flank or belly.
Skins scraped clean, stretched flat
now bear ornate, handwritten accounts
of vineyards, harvests, and fêtes.
Both duke and animal long dead.

Because it wants to, or should culture
and air conditioning fail, the vellum
will return to its original shape,
curl over absent flesh and bone
to reveal phantom muscle memory.
Books could bloom into beasts
tattooed by the vanity of man.

And what of man?
Upright, skin inked
with tigers and sparrows?
Images that do not correspond,
necessarily, to the creatures
that emerge beneath our forms
when we root, rut, and rage.
See the brandished antler,
the bared fang, the nostrils flared
to catch pheromones
or the fabled scent of fear.
Shod in hoof and claw
we shed, at last, language.
Creep into our stubborn animal stories.

Miss Jenny

Miss Jenny was one of our church's widow women,
which meant we gave her most of the deer meat
we hunted and dragged from the woods each fall.
She was somehow related, though the genealogy
was different with each telling.
So some days she was Aunt Jenny, sometimes Miss.
Always, yes ma'am.
I could never imagine her married,
stout as a concrete piling,
feet always planted shoulder-wide,
ready for something unwelcomed, running fast.
I watched her once in our field smoke a cigarette
in between bites of a tomato that she ate like an apple.
Her only nod to gentility
was wiping the pesticide off
on the tail of her dress first.
But she had been married back when
to a long, gaunt man
to this day described in the county
as a kind-hearted soul but
"bad to drink."
Bad to drink.
A sweet, sweet man
who soured on mash
at least twice a month.
Intent on argument and a place
to knock his broad hands,
he often went for Jenny.
But after a while she figured out
that he would follow her,
curses spilling from the corners of his mouth
like tobacco spit.

He followed her around winding up his rage like a toy.
One night she led him yelling to the corn crib
where she pushed him down into his own fumes
to scream, whimper, and cry all night.
This became their custom.
In this memory I do not own,
I see her opening the door
to the crib those mornings,
to her hang dog, hungover man,
restored for a moment
by a wary forgiveness
and a door with a strong latch.

Patient

The first adult to spend the night at Children's,
his only complaints were the snug, duck-print gowns
and the way the nurses talked to him in song
"Like they would to a kid."
The bright red crease in his side
where a kidney was taken for my brother
was not worth mentioning.

Once he walked around for weeks,
face tensed like he was listening
for something, his breath stingy and thin.
When he finally told us how the jack
had slipped and that the truck
had only "bounced a little" on his chest,
the x-rays testified against him
in broken calcium speech.

No matter how many times I asked my brother,
he explained it the same way.
"He just threw up and staggered a little.
I told him to quit, but he just rested a minute,
had a Coke and went back to work."
The second heart attack struck that night
in the ER after Mom insisted they go
because he looked "peaked."
"Still," he bragged, "I laid
three hundred brick after that first one."

That night in the waiting room, my sister
and I huddled against the chilled air.
All night our heads pendulumed in fear
searching the ceiling for our father's
death and its patient, staying hand.

The Ghosts of My Grandparents Visit Me at Work

Grandma keeps petting the red blanket on my chair,
microfiber having arrived well after she left.
"Ain't it soft?" she marvels, and strokes it like a cat.
Papaw studies the basket of woods-walk trophies on a shelf—
feathers, a deserted nest, rocks, a buckeye.
He shakes his head, smiling that I bring such things indoors
the same as when I was half-boy.
"Now what is it you do again, hon'? Grandma asks.
I try to explain the letters behind my name,
how they permit me to make a living by sitting in a room
with people who talk about their troubles.
She nods with a smile like a half-drawn shade,
"But 'Chelle, don't they have any people?"
"They do and for many that's the problem," I joke.
Her mouth drops open and she flickers, fades a bit.
She grabs her purse tight to her like a flotation device.
Papaw looks at me hard but never speaks,
but I know he has diagnosed
most people with either sorriness or meanness.
He lays out his intervention strategy—long rows
of corn, crowder peas and onions to tend and put up.
"Some folks just need something to keep them out of trouble."
I know he is talking of people who hurt others
and that meanness covers everything
from mild rudeness to murder.
It arises from not having a good day's work
behind you at bedtime.
But there are others, I say, so sad you wouldn't believe,
laid out with it, sick with it. He turns to Grandma
and she tells me of her remedies.

First, take a drink of cold water from the tin dipper
by the sink, then pull still-warm eggs from the hen-boxes,
pluck figs from the tree, rock in a chair out front while her
    medicine
cooks—skillet bread and greens with pot liquor, pot roast,
    ice-box pickles,
hummingbird cake and tea.
Take by mouth. Take sleep instructions from chickens.
Fall asleep to cicada song in the room closest to the pantry
with its jeweled walls of plenty pulled from the garden,
a canned wall of comfort
between you and what ails you.

Play-Party, Play-Pretty

It is fatal to be a man or woman pure and simple: one must be a woman manly, or a man womanly.

—Virginia Woolf

From a late '60s book of "play-party" games,
a list of instructions:
"Strike a match.
Pick up a coffee mug."
If you struck the match away from you,
you scored as womanly;
if you lifted the mug by the cup
instead of the handle, manly.
Hilarity ensued depending on how well
or poorly your actions matched your chromosomes.
Gender purity as parlor game.

Much later, a study measured
the discomfort of subjects asked to communicate
with an approaching human figure
whose gender, among other traits, was obscured.
Without the hook or handle
of "her" or "sir," subjects faltered,
unsure of how to pitch their language.
It was called positioning.

Oh, get your mind out of the gutter.
This is not about sex, or is it?
Can life really be one drawn-out version
of that game high school boys used to play,
"Fuck, Marry, or Kill,"
or is it something more?

Maybe one day we will look
at our binary ways and laugh.
Children will marvel that we ever saw gender
as more than a play-pretty, a costume party.
We will finally play well with others,
even when the Other is within our varied selves.

Static

You burst in full of hot laughter frosted
in the night air. Frozen stars lit the crow-wing
shine of your head. When you shook snow
from your shoulders I remembered my father.
Some nights he brought rain home in his hair.
His kisses glazed my forehead with cool shine
while I counted goose bumps into sleep.

A tiny blue spark licked from your fingers
to the doorknob. We both squealed at the snap.
As you leaned in for a kiss I thought
I smelled ozone, tasted tinsel. Shivered.

Every night since I have put on wool socks,
the green Shetland sweater you like,
and the knit cap you left behind.

I have walked heavy and slow, dragging
your absence along the carpet,
then gathering you up again with
each electric nip at the door.

Delta Lullaby

Let me hide you in the country
away from the mosquito whine
of work and want. I will replace
traffic tide with cricket song.
Let me wrap you in a blanket
of kudzu and trumpet vine,
swaddle you in pulled bolls of cotton.
I know the many names and shapes
of poison plants and will distill
their breath into a lethal perfume
for your monsters. I will rock and croon.
No harm will come. Gaze with me
into a waterfall of fading light.
You see how distance fades,
how everything is close and vanished,
near and away? Let the blueing light
lie like moth dust on your eyes.
The dusk is a quilt of bluebird wings.
There is no need to hide. Hush, now.
From a hollow I will watch
you crack your carapace and walk
into the safe and sober day.

Drought Love

The hydrangea wilted every afternoon,
shone blue like a bruise against the trailer
which cut a white two-by-four
between the stripes
of blonde pasture, blue sky.
The husband called the water witch
after a neighbor caught
the wife stealing trough water.

Rented trailer, inherited land,
passalong plant. Grey water
for the tomatoes and corn, water thieved
from horses for the eye-blue flowers.

For thirteen days no real baths,
just washcloth wipings at crotch and groin.
When he came to her, mouth sweet
from a baking soda scrub, the stink
from the rest of him made her swallow.

She whined and laughed as he pushed
her onto the bed, into her own smell.
She—crushed vine, chive, and peat moss.
He—goat and gathered smell of meat.
Together, the crystalline sting of sweat,
mineral heat. They were matter,
matted together on a hand-me-down mattress.

After, they held hands and greeted the dowser,
watched the green Y of the peeled branch
shiver in his hand.

He ducked his head,
hunted the thread of water.
The couple watched him walk,
bob and pause, grumble
when he lost the vein.
He was flustered, all afternoon,
downwind of them.

From the Last Weekend

I did not want it to mean something, the rain. Not this way.

You kept saying, "Can't unring a bell."
Like that means something.

I have been dropping things all day.
As always, helpless at dusk.

I fell for you because you quoted Berry by persimmon light.
The sugar-thick globes like Japanese lanterns.

Don't come at me like that. Not that way.
Your mother told me you slept with balled fists, cheekside,
    even as a baby.

I like my men tender and my women a little mean.

That crow barking over our heads. Heckler.
The weathermen called for rain, but it only threatens.

The braided light at your feet.
The fog plaited in the weeds, along the fencerow.

"A whistling woman and a crowing hen . . ."
Said that every single time.

I blinked pictures of you while the car warmed up.
The open book in your lap, eyes way off beyond the treeline.

The Great Divorce

We have trespassed against our God, and have taken strange wives of the people of the land: yet now there is hope in Israel concerning this thing. Now therefore let us make a covenant with our God to put away all the wives, and such as are born of them, according to the counsel of my lord.

—Ezra 10:2–3

It was the twelfth day of the ninth month,
a day of rain upon rain,
when we gathered to hear Ezra
talk about foreign wives as if we were not there.
Then the sons of priests made confessions
of what had been our vows,
and planned to send us away.
Now, a month later,
after their small offered mercy
of waiting until the rains stopped,
it has taken two days' travel
to lose sight of Jerusalem.
Adara, seven months heavy, claims
to smell their incense fires still,
to taste the rank smoke of burnt ram.
Hana spits so often at the mention of Ezra
that she squats panting in the dust
like a heat-struck ewe, her eyes
locked on a face no one can see.
That first night some of us
buried our idols in fear in shame.
others pillaged the camp,
seeking out Astarte dolls
and fertility stones, late
to please the Nameless One.

"Fools," Hana said,
"as if that will bring him back."
No one is certain if she meant
a husband or a god.
I sit with the old ones,
with jaws like potshards,
set against some loss too bitter to speak.
One remembers her young bride-self
shaking ankle chains at her Levite,
how his eyes glowed at the dances
she learned for the goddess.

At nightfall it is my turn for watch,
and I settle near the edge of camp and listen.
On one side the penitent ones
have gathered for worship, keening
and clumsy at their sacrifices, having
never been taught by their priest-husbands
what happens behind the temple curtains.
On the other side, some women have started
to dance and chant, and make cakes for
The Queen of Heaven.

On both sides, the crying of children.
As for me, I will hide here on this rise,
wrap myself against the night air,
with my back to Jerusalem,
watching the women's camp for
any movement, any sign of
a god that sees.

The Letter

The boy dropped weight through the spring.
While everything else swelled and greened,
he hung in his clothes like a scarecrow.
"Boy, you wouldn't scare away a horsefly."
His father swung his head like a pendulum.
His mother made foods familiar and strange to tempt him.
His sisters fattened as he waned.
"Puny" became his name.
He was not lazy or wormy, as they thought.
His cheekbones shone in his face like a saint's,
not for God or the devil, but lovesickness.
By October he was shunned by all but blood-kin
and even they treated him as a contagion. He read
from the encyclopedia, drew in secret for days,
gathered scrap boards, string. Before the harvest,
he went out after dark and started writing
his love letter in secret, in the far-most field.
With a stake and a long rope, he hemmed the margins,
tramped the edges down, with a hybrid sound
of snapping dry stems and bolls puffing flat.
With boards tied to his shoes, he pressed the stems
down in rounded shapes, using a map he'd drawn:
The Sea of Serenity, The Sea of Crisis.
Two dark circles in a bobbing sea of cotton.
The long teardrop of The Ocean of Storms
left him winded and damp, scratched bloody,
tended by cotton balls with no medicine on them.
He continued, trimming blossoms
to make the shapes of craters and ridges,
trampling whole plants to darken lakes and seas.
As night fell and the harvest moon rose,
he stretched out in one of the seas
to watch her wide face sink into the horizon.

The Going Away

And he said, Go. And he sent her away for two months: and she went with her companions, and bewailed her virginity upon the mountains.

—Judges 11:38

This party sucks.
Her daddy sent us up the mountain
with a band and a banquet,
but nobody will dance.
Not a boy in sight.
What did he expect?
And all she does is cry.

Over there with her favorites.
We're not really close friends,
but that's just because I
called her an army brat once.
My sister Caira is more her age,
keeps pinching me because
I won't make myself cry.

Not a single boy here,
just old musicians and servants.
Caira pinched me good when
I said Jephthah didn't look so tough
when we left, big army man
laid flat, drunk and crying,
while his men were still high-fiving
over their big win.
Our dad drunk with them.
Maybe just a "low infantry man"
like she said, but not a gambler like Jephthah.

Not dumb enough to bet God
for the first thing up the drive.

Caira's just faking to fit in,
but it won't work.
Just like dad said that Jephthah could lead
all the armies from sea to sea and it
wouldn't make him any less a bastard,
wouldn't make his brothers take him in.
It's all so stupid,
and that's why
I won't cry.

The Gideons

for the brethren

Once a year we could count
on a short church service
Because the Gideons would come.
Usually three of them,
squarish in their suit jackets, balding.
Clearing their throats
to be heard over both window units
which roared in their honor.

Instead of preaching, they
told us of their mission and passed out Bibles—
green for college students,
white for medical professionals.

One Gideon raised up a
brick-heavy navy blue hotel Bible,
and talked about the wayward traveler
who stole then later returned it with a note
thanking the Gideons for his salvation.

The reformed thief also included a check
to buy more Bibles so the Gideons
could hide Jesus in nightstand drawers
like an Easter egg.
Even our little church could be
an important part of the Gideons' work,
with a donation, no matter how small.
I went up to them after church to volunteer.

Back then I was a hummingbird-hearted witness,
asking strangers in waiting rooms and grocery lines
if they knew Jesus Christ as their personal savior.

The Gideons told me, kindly, that I
could not pass out Bibles,
but that I could make breakfast for
the nice young men who did.

I do not remember what else was said,
beyond my mother hushing me,
fingernails in my arm.

I do remember what they looked like,
those tidy, cinder grey men,
hands clasped over the thing
I needed, but did not have,
in order to pass out Bibles.

Kept

My aunt's reddest girl stayed outside at reunions, sat closest to the doors at church. She never came back in once she met him, all of us swallowing against his red-wasp colored hair and copper eyes. The devil's nephew lived in a rusted Airstream by a dead pond the color of verdigris. Back-taxed into the no-road woods, he took our girl. Kept the nails on his right hand long, mica chips that sounded like wind chimes made of baby teeth when he played guitar. My cousin said when she slept with him it was like being an abandoned field rooted by razorbacks. For weeks after we got her back she smelled of pine knot kindling, blood bait, and ash.

The Bouffant

Back home, back then, girls were taken
to backyard sheds primped into beauty shops.
The ones with names like "The Hairport"
or "Curl up and Dye."

Beauty shops, like mechanic's shops,
with soft, round women
raising up hair in southern damp and heat.
In the chemical fog of perms and peroxides,
under the constant stage whisper of Aquanet,
they made miracles.

Styles measured in pounds per square inch,
measured in height. Translucent meringues
of hair going up and up.
Coifs of devotion, as Dolly supposedly said,
"The higher the hair, the closer to God."

My mother and I fought the battle
of hair do vs. hair be.
My hair wanted to be left alone,
to respond to wind and gravity,
to be touched.

I have kept my heathen hair,
though tempted last year when I saw,
at the Chinese buffet on the highway,
a waitress wearing a beautiful brown bouffant.
I imagined her carrying smells home in her hair,
a small atmosphere of moo shu fumes and sesame oil.
Later, cracking it under the shower,
the dome melting down her neck.

Her wrapping a towel around her head
in the shape of the hairdo it replaced.
In bed, over the man she loves, taking the towel
down, letting the wet hair fall over him,
around him,
like a blessing,
like rain.

To a Tick

How do I not find you,
little hitcher,
until I get home?
Riding a red seam
where my clothes pressed me,
there you rest, and dine.

Tick, we have only just met
and already I need more space.
I want to talk about boundaries
and you want to talk about need.
Oh, you do give me an itch I can't scratch
mainly because of where you've latched.

Little leech, little teacher,
what do you have to say about intimacy?
Am I willing to listen?
Though I am repulsed,
until I pull you off
we share the same pulse.

A Man's World, 1966

Based on Diane Arbus' photograph "James Brown at home in curlers, Queens, N.Y., 1966"

The woman just out of the frame
could be adjusting a wreath or crown
from the way your eyes roll up
under the weight of some blessing
or coronation, some syncopated call.
Good God!

Instead, your attendant takes out
a series of yellow and pink hair curlers
before shaping that righteous bouffant.
The broad Apache cheekbones cup the light
and your face tilts like a saint's.
Watch me!

The dark spindrift of hair and full mouth,
the heavy torso of a kouros under the Japanese robe.
I don't know karate but I know cuh-razy!
It takes a lot of man to be this pretty.

Not yet the white noise of the crowd,
not yet the hot lights or the banshee cries
that come from a place
not even you recognize.
There's still time to hear the sound of
a theater holding its breath,
the popgun snap of chairs folded shut and
stacked, cramped wallflowers shunned
off the still drumhead of the floor.

Until then, your dresser breathes and hums
around the bobby pins in her mouth.
She is barely heard over the
phantom music of the set list in your head.
You run the changes and tumble
the songs like dominos, like dice, like coins.

Circular Breathing

for the band

I get to pick the warm-up tonight,
so it's "All Blues," my favorite Miles.
The bass player starts too slow,
and before I come in he whispers,
"You'll suffocate, C.," and smiles.
Thinks he's smart cause
bassists don't have to breathe.
At least not to make their
high-strung wooden girls sing.
They only use fingers and bows
to sift sound from the air.
I don't care.
Got the perfect reed tonight.
I love all the sounds that
no one else can hear—
the cat tongue rasp as I wet my Rico #4.
The "peck, pock, poke" of shutting
the right hand keys of my horn.
That second of wind before
the vibration catches in the reed
and falls down the brass.
That bass player can
Kiss. My. Ass.
We call the drummer Take, and he
stirs the dry snare head with brushes.
Jim burbles a low trill while he eyes
a clot of drunk college boys. He hushes
them with a mean, mean face
while his trumpet snarls.

Then he nods to me, inviting:
"C'mon, now."
I pick up the melody, like a mama
with a baby, gentle and firm.
Eyes closed.
This is not a skill as much as
something that my body knows.
I turn the tune in my lungs and mouth,
into my horn and then out.
Through the smoke rings that float stage-side.
The fratties are gentled now, just ponies
with full bellies, still and open-mouthed.
I look at the bassist as I hold the final note,
watch his eyes water before I ever need to blink,
before I look for eyes in the crowd, thirsty to drink
what I pour and pour and pour for them.

Plank

Tuesdays, 3:30 belonged to Curtis.
Nickname "'Tis." He was thirteen,
slim and limber as a vine,
but freighted with man-sized hands and feet.
He spoke up-tempo but diminuendo
so that when I asked "excuse me?"
he mumbled secrets to his collarbone.
So I asked him to play, "Give me a G."
It was not G for gorgeous or grand
or gritty. It was G for gasp,
barely a ghost of a tone.
I took apart his saxophone
to look for loose springs,
a cleaning rag in the neckpiece,
or homework stuffed in the bell.
But it was the reed—a ragged slip
of splinters, a paper doll's broom.
As I reached for a sale box of reeds
he spoke, just that once, forte,
"I don't have money."
"That's ok," I lied, "We have extras,"
and gave him a two-and-a-half.
 He pushed out a braying
honk that made us both jump, and him grin.
The three was a little better, but the tone strayed,
lab-puppy loose and rambling.
At three-and-a-half the room and our ears
rang with it, this small boy's big voice.
That was the reed strength
my friends in college and I used,
and 'Tis was already pushing it
to the edges of itself, pushing the note

to the loudest point before disintegration.
I wonder if he kept playing.
If his long fingers were spared
from the lumber mill, if instead his mind trained
along the contrails of music.
I wonder if by now instead of a reed
thin as a baby's fingernail,
he uses a plank of yellow heart pine,
hewn and fastened
to a voice the size of the sky.

Homa

for Sally Speed

(A *homa* is an ancient Vedic ceremony in which offerings are cast into fire. The offerings become both sacrifice and message. It can be performed to bless, to purify, to protect, or to celebrate.)

"*In ancient times the fire sacrifice was an elaborate ceremony that could involve the sacrifice of horses, cows, and goats, as well as . . . gems and other precious items cast into the fire.*"
—Shukavac N. Dasa

In my memory it is like a shoebox diorama, that night we went to The Manhattan after dinner. I barely recognized you outside of work, in everyday clothes, your black-on-black uniform gone. There we were, two little pipe cleaner counselors bent over drinks. Mine a glass thimble of beer, yours a tiny amber bead of scotch. Off-duty helpers, talking shop.

Later, I asked about your paintings and how they came to you. Whenever I talk to painters I feel the same as when approaching horses: one part captivated to two parts afraid. You told me about a woman who (did I hear this right?) wanted to buy and then "trim" your painting to fit above her couch? Then you told me about the house fire.

Agni, the god of fire, is both a deity and a way to address other gods.

Dear friend, I don't know how to make peace with fire, even in poetry, because I was schooled in hellfire before God-is-love. That is why I cannot, even in a pretty piece of writing, make sense of paintings on fire. If I call it a sacrifice of horses, it is beautiful only here, and only in the way that some scars are beautiful.

Or maybe, if you go back and throw something into that house on fire and smudge the ash on your forehead, it becomes a *durga homa*—an offering to remove negative energies. To protect you from the art-blind buyers of art. To make fire-horse gods out of oil and canvas, quick to carry the message that is now and forever being sent in the air, a warning, a promise, a prayer.

Notes for Fire: an Ars Poetica

for Aralee

No fancy starters
beyond paper or leaves.
Or, if you must,
use shards from the amber heart
of a pine stump, buried
until it stinks of resin.

Stay sharp.
Make a spark
to plant under
a tent of dry twigs
made like a house
for a bird's ghost.
Nothing big.

Be patient.
You are building
an engine of light
that makes its own death.

Keep watch.
The sparks and salamanders
will try to lure you away.
Like every true love,
attendance is required
but not too much.
One part fuel,
two parts air.
Salt with silence
as this is no wordy work.

Don't lean too close.
Fire always demands
a sacrifice, like a goddess
of old, remains hungry
and impartial. Will feed
on wood, hair, skin.

No matter how faithful
your tending, she leaves,
knowing love and worship
grow on the threat of absence.

In the cold dark,
she waits, watching you
gather twigs and leaves.

March Babies

for Nancy Kollock

March babies are made of
long wintered wishes unfurled
like fiddling ferns in the greening air.
We have fine hair that catches the wind
like eiderdown and shed wool,
and soft eyes made for cupping
the newly long daylight.

March babies are fluent in breeze
and brook and birdsong.
We dress in gowns
sequined with cherry blossoms,
embroidered with new vines.
We take dance lessons from lambs,
who are experts in routines set
to the percussion of bud-snap and
The low timpani roll of the earth waking up.

People call us gentle,
soft and sweet, that last word hissed
through pitying carnivore teeth.
They do not know the bravery needed
to chance joy in a blood-red world,
what strength is called up to gambol
in new grass and greet each spring
as if it were the first spring.

And so they will never know,
and it is us who pity them
if only for a moment

before gathering up
the ferocious gentleness required
to love this new day
and all that it contains.

Open Letter to a Girl Who Has Nightmares

for Sierra

I heard you had them, too.
Nightmares, fear-sweat slick,
the dark angels that bar you
from your bed.
If you were younger I would point
to the bent shapes that slouch
into your room, I would show
you the zippers down their backs,
help you hear them rehearsing
their monster scales, coughing
with fatigue and disinterest.

But you are probably too old for that
and wary enough to believe part
of what they pour in your ears
like black sand each night.

But try this. They are night-mares,
ill-tended ebony horses that canter
just within range of the night-watcher lights
around your house.
     Wait,
walk just to the light's edge,
notice more than the red eyes,
the sound their hooves make,
like rocks on gravestones,
like thunder over hollow ground.

     Look
at their ribs, shining black and grey

in the moonlight. In your pocket I have hidden
these charms: plug tobacco, sugar cubes,
and peppermints. Place the offerings
in the flat of your palms made to mirror
the shape of their muzzles. Though
the noise is terrible and you can feel
the strength of their teeth, know
that you have bought their compliance
because of their hunger, because
of your strength.
And even if they wander
into the light of your yard,
your room, they have made
an agreement and know
the shape and scent of your hand.

The Winter Carnival
New Haven, Connecticut, 1972

for Matt, in honor of Gennaro DeGennaro

The fried-dough vendor made the most money,
handing steaming, golden discs through the window,
while people in line stole heat from the side of the trailer.
The air was too cold to carry the scent
of red sauce and sugar very far.
Folks unloaded themselves from the Tilt-a-Whirl
with frosted eyelashes and blue noses.
A clump of teenagers punched each other warm
and swore the ice on the rails made the roller coaster go faster.
Wind pouring through the streets gave couples an excuse
to hide their hands in the warmth of each other's coats.
Head hung, the carnival agent counted the same few bills,
watched the same few faces make the rounds.
No one bought lemonade, but the bootlegger
in the black coat poured shots of limoncello and whiskey
for quarters all afternoon behind the animal trailers.
The big cats curled around their own heat in the cage corners,
refusing to rouse even for sausages thrown in by wheedling
     kids.
An hour before closing the mercury dropped further,
the voices of the dozen people left rose
on the strength of drunken bravery. They willed themselves
to remember the story they were walking in.
Promises and proposals were made, and babies, and beautiful
     mistakes.
Legends of inspired impulse that echoed like carousel music.
The bootlegger and his quarters jingled home
under the strobe and throb of starlight and string-lights
duking it out in the December dark.

His wife rubbed his numb ears back to stinging life
as he laughed about Gennaro's best bad idea
and later fell asleep remembering the sight
he would carry for a lifetime—
of clouds of elephant breath,
fogging over Chapel Street.

Home

for Matt

Homesickness resided in the divot
between my throat and my heart
in a lump, egg-sized,
with a yolk the color of a marigold.

For most of my life
I've woken up from nightmares
mouthing the wish to go Home.
A place on no map I've known
but one I can conjure
as easily as water pouring from a spigot.

Ankle-deep in the burr of hen-talk,
I stand with the one I love.
Our dreams are hand-fed, free-range.
Tangible as feathers and feed-dust,
spanning as far as the horizon.
We are broody with the work
of making things, listening
for the egg-tooth tap of becoming.
We collect poems and images
from the nesting boxes still warm,
ticking with life.
My fingers smell of broken tomato vines
and dirt. Later, onions cut for cooking.
Something simmers in the kitchen,
a recipe from my Mama's side.
I work hard at dusk, memorizing
the black construction-paper cutout
of treeshapes against the sunset.

There are stretches of a backyard
in Arkansas where I could chalk
the exact placement where every puddle
would lay, should rain fall for long.
Yet still less familiar than this plateau of shoulder
and levee of chest that makes up my favorite place
in the world.

Dear One Loved, until the chickens
come home to roost, let me lie down here,
at Home at last.

About the Author

Autobiography in a List of Containers

At first, thimble small, sneaking in,
born with no more weight than a good-sized catfish.
Delivering doctor marked, "lusty cry."
The smallest of the Russian stack dolls
kept in a plastic box pumped full of oxygen.
(They called it an Isolette.)
Every cry bounced back like dock-water waves,
a first lesson in listening.
Held up for inspection through the glass,
just enough baby to hold
a ghost of a miscarriage, the dream of a family.
Grew into a communion cup,
with glass so thin one was tempted to bite it,
mix real blood with symbolic.
Take. Drink.
Cup to bucket, five gallon then ten-, swung between rows
of Bradley County Pink tomato vines
the syncopated thump of the fruit dropped in
under a shallow dish of sky pouring down narcotic heat.
As a teen, the foam lip of outsized earphones
filled up and emptied out music—
contraband, non-country, non-gospel,
David Bowie, Hall and Oates, Prince.
The bell of a saxophone calling out havoc and harmony,
but the sound couldn't reach
through the chlorinated well of the baptistery,
where they held drowning practice in the name of the Trinity.
Adulthood was sipped from a coffee cup, a shot glass.
In a fight, the four-chambered fleshy container
always beats the fissured, boney one up top.
Eventually, there will be a room of Arkansas dirt,
a basement apartment of sorts surrounding

one last container, design as yet unchosen.
Until then I want to rest herein a curvature made of
    hammered brass,
small but heavy, patina'd to the color of brandy.
Attuned to a new-found joy, held in a palm
and the edge circled 'til it thrums,
a shaking felt before the waves cohere.
This is the sound of a singing bowl.

Acknowledgements

Acknowledgements

Grateful acknowledgement is made to the editors of the following journals and anthologies in which these poems, or earlier versions of them, appeared:

Bellemeade Books: "Woman on Fire"
The Chattahoochee Review: "Dissecting the Angel"
Poemeleon: "Circular Breathing"
The Southern Poetry Anthology, Volume V: Georgia: "A Man's World, 1966"
Umbrella: A Journal of Poetry and Kindred Prose: "Static," "Delta Lullaby"
Word of Mouth: "Circular Breathing," "Miss Jenny," "The Winter Carnival," "Woman on Fire"

I offer most heartfelt gratitude to Kathy Prescott and Grady Thrasher, without whom this book would not have been possible. Since we've met, you have been my champions, cheerleaders, and most of all, friends. I am ever grateful for all those gifts.

To David and Donna at Miglior, thanks for being so enthusiastic about the book.

For poetic instruction, inspiration and encouragement, thanks to Judith Ortiz Cofer, for accepting me into her creative writing workshop my last semester of school. You said, "Keep writing." I did. For Kevin Young and the Tin House '09 poetry workshop. For Travis Wayne Denton and the community workshops at Georgia Tech. The community of Athens Word of Mouth inspired and heard many early variants of most of these poems. What a beautiful, mad bunch of muses. You are my home-church and I owe particular thanks to Aralee Strange, Kathy Prescott, Grady Thrasher, Alx Johns, Ciera Durden, Jay Tuco Morris, Mark Pentecost, Bob Ambrose, Stephen Kuusisto, Andrew Mandelbaum, Lemual "Life" LaRoche, Ralph LaCharity, Sandy Berry (for telling me about Word, thanks again), Patrick Conley. David Oates at Wordland, Mark Bromberg at Bellemeade Books. Many more, unnamed but appreciated. To Mrs. Earnestine Ferrell, my high school English teacher, who had us memorize poetry, and kept a poem I wrote for many, many years.

For support of various stripes: Anita Blaschak, my colleagues and friends at Family Counseling Services, Inc. (especially you, John Lee), Linda Estile, Luciano Horescu, Wyler Hecht, C., Lisa Mende. Kenneth Kase, Bill and Miki McFatter, Nicole van Sant, Maxim Eremine, David Noah, Michael Meteyer, and Claire Nichols Zimmerman. To Sarah Jane Bloom, my sisterfriend and oldest poetic co-conspirator. Send poetry.

To my family and kin of every kind. Thank you for your love and support. Especially to my parents, Tommy and Mable Castleberry, who taught me better than to use some of the language in this book, but are still proud of me despite that fact that I did. To my sister, Gina Gregson, for your ever-ready kudos, thanks. Same to little brother, Tommy, Jr.

To Matt. Thank you for your inspiration, joy, love, for "all the time in the world." All my heart—yours. I am the lucky one.

A Note on the Type

This book is set in Adobe Garamond Pro, a digital typeface designed by Robert Slimbach and based on the type of Claude Garamond (c. 1480–1561). A native of Paris, Garamond was a publisher, type designer, and punch cutter whose typefaces are noted for their elegance.